D0679791

BCL: p.744 PS3509

8 50

Poems in Praise

By the same author

*

THE WORD OF LOVE

AMERICAN CHILD

WEST OF MIDNIGHT

ALWAYS THE LAND

WORN EARTH

CORN

BREAK THE HEART'S ANGER

AMERICAN SONG

POEMS IN PRAISE

Paul Engle

RANDOM HOUSE
New York

© Copyright, 1944, 1945, 1952, 1956, 1957, 1958, 1959, by Paul Engle
© Copyright, 1956, 1957, by Botteghe Oscure
© Copyright, 1958, by The Curtis Publishing Company
© Copyright, 1958, by Meredith Publishing Company
© Copyright, 1944, by Dierkes Press

All rights reserved under International and Pan-American Copyright Conventions. Published in New York by Random House, Inc., and simultaneously in Toronto, Canada, by Random House of Canada, Limited.

Library of Congress Catalog Card Number: 59-10822

Manufactured in the United States of America
by the Haddon Craftsmen, Inc., Scranton, Pa.

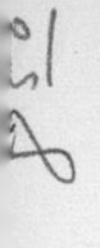

PS
3509
N44P6

ACKNOWLEDGMENTS

The author wishes to make acknowledgment to the following periodicals and publications, in which certain of these poems first appeared:

Better Homes & Gardens
Botteghe Oscure
Cummington Press, for the State University of Iowa
Good Housekeeping
Horizon
Insel-Verlag—*Gesammelte Werke*
The Kenyon Review
Ladies' Home Journal
Life
Living Poetry
Mademoiselle
The New York Times Book Review
Poetry
Qara Press, for the Poetry Workshop,
State University of Iowa
Saturday Review of Literature
Sewanee Review
Virginia Quarterly Review

269119

To A. and M.

High over Ramapo hill
Silent deer still
Jump their gray hoofs over the hearing ground.
Jets over Arden leap with a jeering sound.
Both leave behind them there
Only a sudden marvel of moving air.

Now, like the tracks of deer,
These words the eye can hear
Scatter their signs for wonder, riot, rage,
Over the quiet page.
Those planes fly upward in their praise of blue.
These poems cry upward in their praise of you.

CONTENTS

IV IN PRAISE OF PLACES

V IN PRAISE

IN PRAISE

Praising is all. To live in fright or rage
Is simply to endure and not to live.
Earth praises us by saying, You are here.
Earth's air surrounds us like a second skin
Where light-years bring their glittering caress.
The child's hand lifts. Stars beyond time explode.
The green grass brings the summer and our life.

Praise first the honest sun, which each day dares
To rub across our face its lurid glow.
Face mean, daft, marvelous, dear human face,
Ranting in rages, luminous with love,
You bare your teeth in laughter as in grief.
Porous as limestone, from your mortal eyes
Bubble the living waters of your sight.

Round apples praise by turning plain air red.

Praise comic, dough-shaped nose which, like a dog
Sniffing the odorous, dark wind, discovers
The crust of bread with its brown-smelling wheat.

Praise evil, teaching us to earn our good.

Next praise those hours of total terror when,
The black light trembling, at long last we feel
Fanged sleep pad in and stroke us with its fur.

Praise, too, the charming vanity of girls
Who totter on absurd heels down the street,
Their lovely ankles bent, their round rumps rolling.

Praise words whose vowels and clicking consonants
Grunt, hiss, wail, sing that human noise which means
The mad marvel and furious filth of life:
Words cool to red tongue's touch as the red heart
Of sand-slope melons on a burning day;
The liquid word for water, the soft cry
Called love, at which the solid body shakes;
Those words of wise intensity that make
A spontaneity of formal sound,
Poetry's sensuous, warm common speech.

Lips clench to name the hideous sound for hate.
Mouth flutters as it cries the squeak of fear.
We bite the words for buying, working, weather.
On days when we breathe in our hope like air
Praise the clear syllable that means, to praise.

Praise pain that makes us shudder, more alive,
And prods us into trusting pleasure more.

Praise preachers in their candor who declare
Man is a crude and miserable mote
Waiting to be plucked from God's great eye.

TV, newspapers, radio, all scream
That men and women are a radiation
Of atoms from the deadly blaze of time.
Until the quick explosion of their end
They walk by an odd leaping of the legs,
And love with a hysteria of hands.

We live, they say, like the mad hunter, who,
Driving small game through the deep grass, looks back
To find that he, downwind, is hunted by
The bold and stinking beast of his own death.

Yet praise our death which gives our children life
And death, and gives their children life and death,
Forever children dying into life.

Now tears are poised and ready in our eyes.
Fear tickles like a joker at our nerve.
Earth turns. We breathe. The child cries for our hand.
We give that hand in desperate delight.
It holds us steady where we live within
The round wound of the world, from which we praise.

I

In Praise of People

TO PRAISE A POET:
Robert Frost

I

You give this man the sort of praise
You give to ripened autumn days
When the air glows with radiant light
And leaf fires darken the dense night.

He reads our life. We read his book,
Seeing his own eyes' luminous look
Gleam from the poem, knowing behind
That inky page a shining mind.

The falling red leaf silently
Proves the standing maple tree.

When he says *star,* we make a wish.
When he says *lake,* we watch live fish,
The water moving with their motion.
When he says *salt,* we taste the ocean.

Independent animal,
Stubborn individual,
He makes his way, and has from birth,
With or against obstinate earth,
Trudging, like a man through snows,
Leaving deep footprints where he goes.

His shadow, folded like a fan
Over the pavement, casts a man.

Like a New Hampshire apple growing
Ripe in the sun and green winds blowing,
Or painted, and about to roll
Out of Cézanne's red-painted bowl,
Pushing the green air back, his face
Brings with it his own light and space.

A sugar maple, sweet and hard,
He stands up in his own back yard,
Taking the sunlight eagerly,
Rooted in rough integrity.

Aware, the honest poem is no
Romantic cry, because tears flow,
He lays with calloused hand each thick
Word on word like brick on brick.

Aware rich soil is grit ground fine,
That the same voice can sing or whine,
He knows in evil we define
Good, as tears make our eyes shine.

Stargazer whom no star deceives,
Shrewd skywatcher who perceives
The midnight moon bark at the prowling
Mongrel dog and send him howling;
Farmer who heard the rattler warn
From the stone ledge his angry scorn,
Hears from their coiling length the bright
Galaxies hiss their golden light,
And in that instant hears the high
Shrill from low grass of cricket cry.

Earth or sky or mortal heart
He travels without map or chart,
Or any compass but his art.

Loving the marvelous human scene
Where the absurd grins at the mean,

Knowing the mixed magnificence
Of all life's sensual innocence,
He mingles vision with plain sense:

On this wind-rounded world the bare
Loved face hangs like a bruise in air.
We lift our hands to touch it there.

If that touch brings pain with delight,
Joy so great as to give fright,
It is our life, and it is right.

Love is not wages to be earned,
Nor lessons to be grimly learned,
But a grace given and returned.

II

Maple, granite, Frost the man,
Name better substance if you can.

Essential character that changes
Like his New England mountain ranges,
Dark green by day, black green by night,
Turning to green the changing light.

Thirsty as any mortal caught
In the dry sands of abstract thought,
He turns from Plato's pure ideal
To drink the cold spring of the real,
Proving by his devoted act
Enchantment of the daily fact.

He knows the apple tree puts forth
Its best fruit planted to the north,
On slopes where rock and thin grass meet
(But grass between the stones is sweet).

Sore head, sap head, bleeding heart,
All these he knows are simply part
(As in one body: gut, brain, knee)
Of our contrary symmetry.

Sturdy Monadnock of a man,
He lifts, as mortal courage can,

Through years too coarse yet too refined,
A high green mountain of a mind.

Practical countryman, through fields
He walks, and estimates the yields,
Or leaves, down city streets in rows,
Poems like seedlings as he goes.

Shy man who planted trees, he knows
(Windbreak to storms of men and snows)
A wood of wit, in his defense,
Hides natural intelligence.

Rockets rise where none have flown;
He mends his wall with fallen stone.
Man-made stars flare into birth;
He sees ants drag their crumb of earth.

We calculate the flaming run
Of satellites around the sun,
But the most human width of space
Is breadth across his living face.
Time is the brilliant impetus
Of light-years burning; but for us
Time is the day we wait for, when
Such a poet comes again.

He knows how, having held his mare
Still, in the loud and burning air,
Blacksmiths, below their smoky roof,
Fit the hot shoe to the cold hoof.
Himself a singer, he knows how
The toughest fields polish the plow,
The branch gives lightness to the bird,
The poem gives brightness to the word.

The poem, we hear his calm voice say,
Is but a momentary stay
Against the frantic world's confusion,
Letting hope live in disillusion.

He knows how the deliberate snail
Leaves on a leaf its shining trail,
How common sense, uncommon rage,
Shudder the poem across the page.

Pacific to Vermont he went,
Striding in strength a continent,
Now all the states between rejoice
To see his face and hear his voice,
A live man bringing, north and south,
More life out of his speaking mouth.
Unhurried, free, with steady gait
He is our greatest, final state.
In him these crooked times provide
A straight astonishment of pride
In such a country, when it can
Bear such a poet, such a man.

CHARLES BAUDELAIRE:

Montparnasse Cemetery, 1867

(Centennial Ceremony, Publication of Les Fleurs du Mal, University of Iowa, 1957)

Reader, pity if you can
Your likeness, that self-pitying man
For whom the world was opposite,
The happy man a hypocrite.

From that contrary human fight,
The left hand snarling at the right,
God and Satan battling in
Man's soul with fists of love and sin;
From blessed peace and bitter rage,
The flowers and cities of his age,
From the disorder of his senses,
From shattered nouns and troubled tenses,
The prayers, the cries of love, the curses,
He made the order of his verses,
From beauty and brutality
A terrible morality.

Absurdly, wisely, purely human,
He knew that sinful man and woman
In knowledge of pure evil sense
The form of primal innocence.
Société des Gens de Lettres
Sent no dry member for that wet
Funeral, to mitigate
Respectability's scared hate.

When the hearse came with its proud weight
Thunder shook, to celebrate,
The iron cemetery gate.

For the gold francs that they could save,
They put him in the same tight grave
With Aupick, strict and honorable,
Stepfather, hero, general,
Who bravely faced at Waterloo
British and bayonet, who knew
With expertness the expert gun,
But not this dangerous, mad son.

Always the dream of voyage, far
Beyond lost island or last star.
But no departure, no arrival,
Only a passive, dread survival.
Each trip to any foreign part
Began and ended in the heart.
Only his own self he explored,
Ruthless, honest, often bored,
Sailing the body's sensual curve,
Sad navigator of the nerve.
But then one last successful trip,
By flowered hearse not outbound ship:
He who had always feared the void
Surely then was overjoyed
To find himself on solid grass,
The peasant mud of Montparnasse.

As his wild heart began its flight
Into the land beyond our sight
Where all is beauty, calm and light,
Over that once ecstatic brain
Fell mocking and voluptuous rain.

TO BE SUNG BY ELEANOR STEBER

Now in a world where dark and light
Quarrel in the heart like day and night,
Where all men hunger for something more
Than fear of fear and fear of war,
I bring you a better thing than wheat
For hand to bake and mouth to eat.
To all the world where all belong
Out of my mouth I bring you song.

Out of the long American land
I bring you song like a loving hand,
Nothing but hope and trust I bring,
A singing mouth for all who sing.
I give you now for all life long
Music, music—I give you song.

WILLIAM CARLOS WILLIAMS, M.D.:

His Seventy-fifth Birthday, September 17, 1958

William Carlos Williams, known as Bill,
Doctor of medicine, man of good will,
Poet who writes in his own natural voice
Praise of the natural world: Now we rejoice
That here among us is a man who sings
Plum, dish, rock, water, ideas-in-things.
He spent his time with the stink of the sick and dying,
But held the baby, too, in its first-air-trying.
Always, whether feeling last pulse or first, giving
Ease to anguish, making life more living.
Like paper messages up the string of a boy's kite
He sent to the world the poems that he could write
Between his patients—tumor, hernia, flu—
Saying I'm here, and this is what I knew
When I saw the round earth like a green bush shaking,
And felt my eyes in that green vision breaking.
Yet this is wrong. He hates meter and rhyme
As worn-out manners of an outworn time.
But let him bear, this once, his agitation,
And join us in a cheerful celebration:
Let each say, Look! I'm lucky to be alive
The day Bill Williams has turned seventy-five.

WILLIAM CARLOS WILLIAMS, M.D.

Bill Williams lives back east in Rutherford, New Jersey
(called in the black of time by the Indians, Boiling Springs,
but the springs are buried now or turned into sewers).
He lives near the civil and hill-rising Passaic River.

I live out in Iowa where the corn leaves shake all summer
beyond the bull-shouldered Mississippi River,
but a lot of people out here know about Dr. W. C. Williams.
He has delivered more babies than any other poet in history—
two thousand, to be exact—dragged into the world
as live and kicking as his own poems. Between mending
bones and bellies and even that soft-tough organ the brain,
he has worked at mending the language.

Read his poems out loud and hear,
beyond and through the broken lines,
the motion of a man's voice speaking.
The live words jump and quiver in the common air.

Bill Williams is a man devoted to the human race,
loving its power for love and meanness, clearly
knowing it has the power to pick your pocket
when you bend down to help as it lies injured,
kicking and screaming there on the stone street.
He didn't get that way by reading books the professors
chop out of each other's knowledge like salt blocks.
He learned by diving into the dark pool of life
as a boy into the pool under the Passaic Falls.
He accepted the whole dirt and the delight of it.

The lure of libraries, calling men to their safe
and feminine caves, has never gentled him.

Like a man wading a rapid river, to keep his footing
he keeps moving.

He has walked the streets of a named city,
feeling the concrete hard under his leather shoe.
Liking the people there, he has not lamented
the quick deer driven back to the Ramapo hills.
In the fret and fume of that place he has done his job
with deft hands, refreshed by his work as other men by play,
a damn good doctor
for all kinds of men and women and their snot-nosed kids.

He does not mourn wildflowers bulldozed into the ditch
for homes with families he visited with his medicines
compounded from gentian, ginseng and digitalis.

He has taken the real world of virus and grass,
of microscope and factory, of the corner wind
blowing dust in his eyes, and made a true vision
of reality out of it. From artless things that
simply stand up hard in the ravaging daylight
in all of their blunt thingness, he has made
a hard and honest art.

He has listened to many voices on American streets,
in stores and hospitals, talking about weather, war,
pains, politics, gossip, and heard that speech
go up and down with a new twist to the old words.

It wasn't English porridge he wanted for breakfast,
but Quaker Oats, made in Cedar Rapids, Iowa,
with a picture of Ben Franklin big on the box,

from grain raised in the long middlewestern bread basket
that runs a thousand miles from the old Appalachians
to the young, rough Rockies.

Like the antibiotics he learned to use, his poems
heal and are healthy.

He is still good for a laugh, driving his wit
like a new nail between anxiety and despair.

He still wants to know men and women so closely
he can look into the whites of their eyes and catch
the flicker of health or illness there, and find
their individual smells with his curious nose.

No vagueness for him as doctor—the disease
hunted, named, fought.

No vagueness for him as poet—always the bright
particulars, as a doctor works with the definite
fever, bone, fear. No universals for him apart
from the precise thing—not the general color of red,
but that exact geranium in its tin can, rusted and red.

He lays his hands on the body of this world,
punching the pain,
finding the cold dread and the warm desire,
the hungry tissue and the voluptuous gland,
the mixed-up rapture, reek and wonder of it.

He writes what he sees, the poet of what is there.
Nothing to be concealed, neither the dark blood
of the internally bleeding gut, nor the white
shadow of love a man and a woman cast in the hidden night.

He has an animal's memory of places: Cholla
seen from a passing train, Paris walked in slowly,
remembering how he went as a boy through all that
shaped stone and the shapeless crowds,
the hills of west Jersey glowing in their greenness,
the halls of the old French Hospital in New York
torn down for the Lincoln Tunnel.

A man of this world, knowing our human hate,
the wildness padding through our mind's civilized jungle,
but still believing in men, women and children,
still trusting our betrayed idealisms, fond of our affections,
hopeful of our hope.

For him, every life is a poem, although few speak it.
He has seen the hunted news in the maimed eyes
of women screaming in childbirth and of men
watching their bodies shrivel as the bloated
cells of cancer grew. To him, they are all important.
They are, after all, people, who suffer their poems
instead of writing them.

A poet, like a doctor, goes to the base and bone of things,
under the words, under the clothes, under the skin,
to find the elemental and lay it bare.
Both want to know life, not as a philosopher holds
ideas cold and clear in his mind as ice cubes,
but to smell it, touch it, taste it, watch it breathing,
hear the valved heart go beating-thud, beating-thud.
For are they not both interested in man?
In the stench of the sickroom, in the horror
of human rage and defeat
that crawl across the face like dripping sores,
they both look for the essential thing

in all its great beauty, freed for a moment
to fly guiltily around the room.

He has made a myth of a real city called Paterson:
its rock and water, its past and present, its people
laughing and bawling and working. He made from that city
the presence and sound of a man talking a live vision.
It is a strange and proud thing for a place on the earth
to have its own legend written in its own lifetime.

Like any of us who has lived long in one town,
he enjoys driving his car on the familiar streets
where he recognizes the big elms and the little dogs,
the wooden houses where he has felt
the forehead flame and the hand go cold, and heard
the child's voice strangle in the filled-up throat.
He waves to the cops on their way to arrest a speeding truck.
He is a man at home in his own home town.

Now he wants to live in a little house
in his own back yard, close to the mess and marvel
of daily, ordinary, dirty life,
where he does not have to write his poems between patients.

There, like a man shaving the same scraped face,
pulling his cheek sideways, he can let the steam of his poems
rise from the warm bowl of his imagination.

There he can delight in the eye colored with looking,
the ear beaten and blessed with the machine roar of our time,
with the lively, pleading, bitter, lovely words
yelled down the streets of his town, the kids
calling each other to come on out for one more day
in the loud, clear sun, to throw, to catch, crying,
Come on, Harry, run with it.

His poems rise in the falling flow of our days,
where the hours splatter and float like foam,
as bass once jumped in the pool under the Passaic Falls,
shining and alive. So they will leap and fall
in their lithe quickness, as the years stream over,
around and under them, as long as men use English
words in the steady flow of an American voice speaking.

PORTRAIT OF A KING'S MISTRESS, NUDE

One sinuous wrist is lifted while it shakes
Golden bracelets in the form of snakes.
The black hair rises in a bird-wing hush.
That belly must have burned the painter's brush.
Her slitted eyes measure the mortal distance.
Lips part against the curved jaw's cruel insistence.
Breasts touch the naked sunlight with a kiss.
Arms stroke the crimson cover with a hiss.
The poured-out skin flows on the couch like milk.
The long legs slither through a field of silk.
The small toes curl in sensual indolence.
The bent knees in their waiting lie intense.
Whole body, lithe limb and fanged head alike,
Coil, ready for the rapturous hour to strike.
Tongue trembles, feeling the voluptuous air.
From hinting hand, the white fanged shoulder's stare,
And from the insolent mouth that smiles above,
She drips the lovely venom of her love.

A king was ravished by those charming thighs.
There were no scales before the painter's eyes.

COLETTE

I

Terrified of moonlight as a child,
Ashamed, as a woman, of her shameless eyes,
For love in them the hot daylight defiled,
How could she be both passionate and wise?
First marriage meant: dull home, hot tea, admire
The man, his tie, his cutlet, like a boy.
Second: a burnt child going back to the same fire
Where it had been once burned—but with what joy!

What leads us, scratched with thorns, back to the past?
We drag it, bawling like a calloused peasant
Dragging a calf, to the market of the present.
Pain or pleasure, some things one cannot flee.
Female I was and this at least will last,
For better or worse, a female I shall be.

II

Every-which-way but not frowzy hair,
A face all shrewd and lively womanhood,
Sometimes an outraged hen with furious glare
Pecking at wolves in the voluptuous wood.
Of men she knew (and young) the best and worst.
Home gave her honor, Paris naughtiness,
Wit she wore like a frock, had from the first
A little weak and human haughtiness.

Love was her land, as some men never rest
Until they cut their handholds in the dark
And final slopes of deadly Everest.
The mortal heart she knew like a modern city,
The stinking alley, the pretentious park,
Where passion lurches arm-in-arm with pity.

III

A country girl corrupted into art
She threw her stories at the world like stones
That tore the breathing skin from the aching heart
And showed live marrow in the brutal bones.
She knew the buzzing of the summer bee
Flying above the sting-invaded flower,
And knew the anguished wait for the loved key
Forcing the lock, hour after hour after hour.

The bestial id, mad for its bloody meat,
She had endured, for even it could bless
Bewildered human living that could join
The soul's ultimate grovel in the groin
With a sixteen-year-old Burgundy girl's sweet
Religious wonder at her first caress,

IV

A face as innocent as a falling leaf,
Sunlight flowing like blood through every feature,
But the same face that later cried in grief:
To throw my arms around the neck of a creature,
Man or dog, who loves me. Living breath
Caresses the lung as a dear hand the cheek.
Not to love is pure, appalling death.
Better to love, be shattered, again to seek.

Look! Intense and dawn-delighting face,
An Eden-earth, turning in fiery space,
To be explored and mapped and importuned,
Desired beyond enduring, gladly taken,
A face to learn its whole life could be shaken
When scars came first and then the bleeding wound.

V

To love again, when one's already savaged
By first betrayal, she wrote, is like the ill
Who think they are cured, but once again are ravaged,
Crying, I thought it was over! Let it kill!
Life's degradation and divinity
She knew, as mechanics know a skilled machine,
And most of all, that mortal trinity:
A man, a woman, and the love between.

They said, She is life-toughened, nerved with steel.
Ah no! she answered, merely made of woman,
But that's enough, feminine, bone-real.
Living was loving, if it had a name,
Even in those most horrible and human
Hours when shrill tears burned her eyeballs like flame.

VI

An arrow of rubies bleeding at her throat,
And indignation sparkling in her hair,
To a young man, in angry love, she wrote:
You beg, share my life. But you mean, Take my share.
Like a hanged man cut down in time to live
I fill my lungs with air and say, Good-bye.
You mostly took while thinking most to give.
I love you, but I want to be an *I*.

Good-bye sticks in the mouth like broken glass.
Under the candid lens of this May light
Coal shovel, hearth and tongs, whatever things
We shared once, now glare at me when I pass.
I want my life, yet now the plain daylight
That touched us both, falls on my skin, and stings.

VII

Person, woman, child, her pride she held
Like a thirsty knife, at the live throat of men,
And sometimes slashed, but when they bled and yelled,
Put them to bed and nursed them well again.
At eighty, lack of love was all she hated,
Bought violets with their earth-dripping root,
Subtle and simple, she was violated
By innocence, as a young girl by a brute.

Curled up like a tamed animal, she said
To him, Take! I wish I could give you more.
Then more than body gave to his embrace.
When death came, she said, Take! And when the dread
Looking glass saw the loved face it bore,
The mirror wept, but not the dying face.

VIII

The picture was a young, old-fashioned girl
Laughing over the trout-enticing water,
With hair that looked one live, exuberant curl:
Dark in the sun, a life-delighting daughter.
Her eyes like swallows, ranging the round air
(Creature herself), watch rapid animals:
Rabbit on grass, butterfly on pear,
Red squirrel hullabalooing on garden walls.

Zoos she loathed, but later had a cat
That leapt like a child in the glory of her age,
A furry fury. Did she learn from that
To scream the purple vowel of pain and rage,
Hearing, half-craved, half-feared, in a city flat,
The lion of love roar from his living cage?

JOSEPH'S SUSPICION

(Translated from Rainer Maria Rilke's "Argwohn Josephs")

The angel spoke and tried to hold
Back the man, and turn his fists away:
Do you not see in every fold
Of her, that she is cool as God's first day.

Darkly the other stared, and tried
Only to murmur, What has changed her so?
Now, carpenter, the angel cried,
Can you not see through this the Lord God go?

Because, with pride, you work in boards, will you
Blame him, bitterly, who well
And modestly out of that same wood grew
Green leaves, and let the live buds swell?

He understood. And as he turned to the quick
Angel his actual, terror-given gaze,
It was no longer there. He thrust his thick
Cap slowly off. And then sang praise.

A GIFT OF SONG:

For A.

Most arts are artificial things.
Canvas, bound book, carved stone
Are a shaped silence. Song alone
Is natural when the live voice sings.

Cities in their great smoky wrong
Corrupt the common air,
But singing woman, even there,
Utters the pure, perfected song.

Even while mourning human death
Song brings to the curved ear
Enchanted grief, delight and fear,
Shaped by a living human breath.

Listen! Each absolute, loved note
Soars up, each simple word
Flies like a trained and startled bird
Out of the curved ecstatic throat.

THE NAME OF LOVE

I

In the young years I thought that it was wrong
For love to have a word called *love*, a name
Such as we give to anger, touch, hope, song,
Or a late child we call back home and blame.
I thought love was an eloquence of eyes,
Shudder of breath without a verb, the quick
Huddle of hands, something far too wise
To want a name, as we say: dark, fear, brick.

Now in the middle years I think it right
For love to have a name endured in time,
A live and human sound the teeth can bite:
Like the tongue's limp stumbling over *lame,*
Mouth's hunger calling *bread* like a bell's chime.
I tell the word for love. It is your name.

II

Mademoiselle means slenderness of waist,
Look of eyes and lift of hands nimble as light;
Fräulein is firm on the tongue as beer's taste,
Mellow and malty-brewed and the foam bright;
Signorina flutters from the mouth,
Laughing syllables, leaping the live air;
Señorita glitters with the south,
Legend of red flower in the jet-black hair.

But *Miss* will be the honest English word
For you, as blunt in talking as teeth biting
The ravaged name for love, or fool, or blonde,
A sound as hard as the horn beak of a bird,
A word as plain as a rock dropped in a pond,
Foaming green water, dark, and sun-delighting.

III

Look! The air shudders when you breathe it in.
Never in its cold flight from north to south,
Over hill's height, field's reach, lake's languid skin,
Was such warm substance as your waiting mouth.
The high noon sun clangs in your eyes, a yell
Of purest yellowness. My blue eyes catch
In yours the sound of seeing like a bell.
Your body burns the daylight like a match.

Looking at you, common sense is senseless.
The natural truth of touching is a lie
When hands view visions. Each sense is defenseless
When love deranges simple time so we
Live only in the quick eternity
Between the breathed-in air and breathed-out cry.

IV

A scream of color in a hush of sound,
The cardinal fled from us in his fear,
Singing in his wild flight over green ground
Red song that burned in the astonished ear.
We laughed that such a small and feathered flame
Should have such fright—then heard our own hearts thud.
Innocent face to face was shame to shame.
The sun bled light upon our living blood.

Better, later, in the friendly dark
When night crept by us on its hands and knees
And there was nothing for the eye to mark
But the red silence of the nerve's elation,
That man-with-woman look that only sees
The blackness of the brain's obliteration.

II

In Praise of Children

A CHILD IN EDEN

In Eden once warm wind blew from the east.
The animals who sniffed that innocent air
First smelled live man. Their instinct cried, Beware!
That is a wicked and a dangerous beast.
No claws or fangs, he is another kind,
Who stumbles through this place, upright and slow,
But has a deadly power that does not show,
A cruel and marvelous muscle he calls mind.

Weaker than we, man with that mind knows how,
By using rock and fire, he could destroy us.
But we do not despair, we saw him go
With a small creature yearning to enjoy us.
When it first saw us here, it simply smiled:
A kind and marvelous beast that he calls child.

TO BE A CHILD

Doomed as absurd adults, we can forget
That stories run through children's heads, the way
Young children run all through a summer day,
Hot in the blazing of the alphabet.
We watch her reading there, wearing her wild,
Utterly-given-up, ravenous look.
But see! It is as if a breathing book
Has picked her up and reads the living child.

This is to be a child: To heighten
Each thing you handle, to be shyer
Than rabbit in wide field, to frighten
Deep dark that scared you, to fly higher
Than kite or hunting hawk, to brighten
Daylight, because you are a fire.

YOU CAN'T BE WISE

Denied, she screamed in rage, and ran away.
I yelled. She halted, rigid in her going,
Water frozen in the act of flowing.
Then suddenly her fearful face turned gay,
I'll come right back, she called, and laughed. Like wood
Amazed at turning into violin,
At having such a sweet, wild voice within,
She was amazed at turning into good.

Bright as a fragment of the first creation,
Her hand took mine and I could feel it glow,
For love was in her like a lamentation.
What does a mere man do with such surprise?
Don't punish, give your love, and simply know
Wisdom is knowing when you can't be wise.

THE SOUND OF GREEN

The color red has quick teeth that can bite,
While blue caresses like a friendly child.
Black is a beast that shambles through the night.
Green is the sound of grass, growing and mild.
Gray is the dripping hush of morning rain.
Gold is the song of birds in a tall tree.
Orange is all the noisy hue of pain.
Brown is a rabbit you can barely see.

Purple is our color of apprehension
When she is lost on a white summer day.
We call in voices yellow with our tension.
And then we hear her calling far away
And see, in love, her many-colored cry,
A rage of rainbow arching the clear sky.

THE SOUND OF RED

Like mirrors marvelously lost in mirrors
Her eyes reflect the memories of her day.
Wildly she tells us, ever-eager hearers,
About the bright red fox that ran away
But seemed to leave on the hill a bright red track.
I was so scared I closed my eyes, she said,
And everything got red. We heard come back
A red voice calling faintly, Red! Red!

She stood so radiant in her own fright
The blond air turned the color of her fear,
In which her eyes like little blue suns glared.
But then she cried, too loud, I think I scared
That fox as bad as he scared me. Her tight
Hand clutched mine in the fury of her pride.

BOOK AND CHILD

I

High from these printed, silent sounds, the bird
That carried Sinbad and his diamonds hangs,
Out of this cave of frightful phrase and word
Old tiger roars between his ripping fangs.
Down from the grassy hills of this plain prose
Indian horse and warrior surprise,
The boy hears yells of Gall and Roman Nose
And Custer's yellow hair screams in his eyes.

Battle comes to his bedroom. In his fright
His hands jerk back as if the book would bite.
But goes on reading, takes that book to bed,
By all that verbal violence comforted,
Happy to see, in his devoted rage,
The whole world come alive on that dead page.

II

She tries to read, but words are only jumbles
Of shape that twist her tongue until it clashes:
Long consonants are sticks on which she stumbles,
Round vowels are muddy pools through which she splashes.
Dog is a sound that bristles like a bark,
Cat is a sound that yowls and turns up fur.
But no shape on that page is a real mark
For living animals that play with her.

She throws the book down, her feet start to stamp.
Shocked at her act, she takes it, holds it tight,
Knowing that from these pages, secret, dumb,
Her long-loved story once again will come.
Her eyes fill, not with words, tears, mad, but light.
That book glows in her like a turned-up lamp.

III

Animal stories make the world a zoo
In which the fiercest animal is you.
When the book says, Rain fell and thunder rolled,
They shake, and huddle down against the cold.
But when they turn the page and read, The sun
Came out and all the clouds went, one by one,
They looked up toward the light and smile for knowing
They hold the sky in their hands, blue and blowing.

No fierce ghost prowling through its haunted house,
No golden nymph turned greenly into tree,
No mouse changed into monster, back to mouse,
No spook from caves, no demon from the sea,
Has so intense and wild and lost a look
As children holding in their hands a book.

CHRISTMAS

Inhabited by terrors, like a town
Where mad dogs, foaming up and down,
Moan at the sun as if it were the moon,
Bite the innocent air at noon,
We go to the windows of our eyes and peer
At our own life running in the image of a furred fear.

But we forget, a candle close to the eye
Blinds the sun in the blinding sky;
Forget, hope walked in the body of a Man
This savage earth where life began;
Forget, our children celebrate the day
A child was born to change men's old and brutal way.

In the common bawl and reek of birth He came
Like any boy, given milk and name.
But suddenly a miracle: that blessed
Thin boy nourished the swollen breast.
God in that moment, men knew, proud and wild,
Had said the Word which was the love which was the Child.

In that dark season when all green things die
Christ gave his first live human cry.
Winter that kills the leaf and piles the snow
Brought the small Son of life to grow.
Recall, in the freezing touch of time, men told
That God became a living Child and shook with cold.

Dumb creatures brought the first gift. Cows and sheep
Purely by being there, asleep,

By blowing white breath over their horn feet,
Gave him their animal, blood heat,
By simply standing there alive, transformed
That useful place, blessed Child and barn their bodies warmed.

Now through our cities bells in their rocking motion
Call to this day their bronze devotion.
Now look! The air, as if the great sky fell,
Shakes all around us. Like a bell
Hung out in glittering space, the whole live earth
Swings and rings in the stars to praise one little birth.

III

In Praise of the War Dead

JOHN MAC ALISTER, FLYING OFFICER, R.A.F.

What should a fighting man
Take to his death beside
Powerful anger and
A private inner pride

That he used in one act
Of terrible, clean tension,
Skill of hand, the eye's
Delicate suspension?

Wanting but solid earth,
The friendly look, the bare
Hearthstone's warmth, he died
In the aloof cold air.

He did not train for death,
Practicing night and negation.
By life, touch, love he turned
Athlete of resignation.

What can we say above
Ground for him gone under?
Not prayer, pity, praise,
Nor weeping, only wonder,

Only astonishment
A man of quiet name,
Dark, calm and kind, should die
In fury and in flame.

For life, unplanned, light, free,
Any commemoration
In rigid stone would be
A marble mutilation.

Let us have one intent:
Grow grief in our own face
To be in that live place
A mobile monument.

Not that he was brave,
Left family and friend,
His was a mightier end—
A world grows from his grave.

This frantic fact alone
Defies the sound for sorrow,
We walk into tomorrow
Over his breath and bone.

FOR THE IOWA DEAD

I

On this wall, in this town, in their own state
We name their individual names, to state
That they were not just group, crew, squad, alone,
But each one man, one mortal self, alone,
Who fought the brutal frenzy of his time,
Who touched with human hand this iron time.
We give to them, who died in every weather,
Grief like an old wound groaning with the weather.

They knew death as a family dog knows men,
By whistle, touch, familiar smell of men,
But still were cheerful, still could ask each morning,
What do you know for sure on a new morning?
Before death's final stammer in the throat
Knew love's live stammer in the breathing throat.

II

Some left an office, cornfield, factory,
But these men left the study of mankind,
Glory and gloom of mortal history,
The wonder, madness, logic of the mind,
The live cells, atoms cunningly combined.
They closed their books, death closed their eyes, so we,
The lucky Iowa living, still could find
A future in our human liberty.

The wise and wicked past they came to study,
Right and wrong, life loved like light, but turned
Away from contemplation to the bloody
Present, and in appalling action learned
The old world's furious and deadly fact:
Murder for justice is a moral act.

III

Morning Sun, Stone City, Boone, What Cheer:
In the hysteria of history
These names for home rang in the homesick ear,
With the warm sound of friend and family,
Of Iowa, where winter cracks your skull,
Where summer floats on fields, green river flowing,
Where autumn stains your hand with walnut hull,
Spring shakes the land with a loud gust of growing.

But their true season was the one of dying.
Summer, autumn, winter, spring all ran
Into one flaming moment, doomed plane flying,
Sinking ship, exploding shell, edged knife:
For home is not birthplace, but the place a man
Dares a way of death, to keep a way of life.

IV

Most of their life was simply, to make life:
The clover planted and the cattle bred,
Each year the wheat field ripped by the plough's clean knife,
The crust of earth cut like the crust of bread,
The fat hogs slopped, the ludicrous, loud hogs,
The skimmed milk saucered for the lazy cats,
The careful mating of the hunting dogs,
The oat bin plugged against the ravenous rats.

But then their life changed simply, to end lives:
The strange men killed less quickly than the brown
Beef steer by the sledge and the neat knives,
The child's hand begging but without an arm,
The cattle shelled in the defended farm,
The crazed cat shot for luck in the taken town.

V

Not heroes, angels, merely men,
Strong, weak, as any citizen,
Caught between evil and hard good,
Nail between hammer and hard wood,
Caught between, in that black year,
The hate of hate and fear of fear,
Yet the hard courage they could bring
Made the name *men* a mighty thing.

Like prophets in their innocence
They had their vision of violence,
And found in a shell-shattered place
More than a dead boy's ruined face:
Carved marble Christ head in the mud
On whose cheek stone tears turned to blood.

VI

Some left green meadows for the greener ocean,
Left the low rising, falling of that land
For a more violent and reckless motion
No landscaped brain and body could withstand.
American bones beneath that brutal water
Move in the cold and restless bed of sea,
And have no dream of any woman's daughter
Warm in another bed that will never be.

Darker than earth is the sea-depth where they died,
A bitter grave in a salt and barren place
For those whose loam had made yield after yield.
Their chalk hand twitches but only with the tide.
Now is the lean and cropward-looking face
Gone from their skull like soil from a gullied field.

VII

Say that in the end their life was one
Quick autumn burning the leaves with their own blood,
Say that they fought so there might be the sun
Over their land, as they died in the mud.
Not from an abstract sense of wrong and right
But for the hill they fenced with aching arm
They went to the unwilled war—and wrote one night,
It's a lousy land and a hell of a way to farm.

Say that for those who came from corn and flock,
By inland rivers where the catfish hang
In the dark pool, and the moccasin hides its fang,
Where the warm milk is cooled in the old gray crock,
It was a tough, hard, bitter death as they sprang
And poured their rich blood over the barren rock.

VIII

Now in a later year
When sky on farm and town
Bleeds furious daylight down
On faces bleeding fear,
Let hope like a great blaze
Rise when we speak the name
Of those who died in flame.
Take pride in simple praise:

Brave, bitter, or afraid,
They won their appalling fight.
Eternal sun has laid
Its bending arm of light
Over their shoulder blade
And burned them into night.

IX

Some chose to fight above the bloody ground,
Above the keel-carved sea, a high third way.
They measured murder on a map, and found
Accurate death dropped from the bright bird-way.
Loathing destruction, they were great destroyers.
Flyers who wanted only to walk again
As merchants, farmers, teachers, salesmen, lawyers,
They brought an air-borne death to earth-borne men.

They flew to kill and some of them were killed.
They bombed the concrete fort and broke the city.
They turned their armed, trained face to the enemy.
Nothing is to be pitied here but pity.
They did their job and saved a state. Their skilled
Hands are shattered into history.

X

Do not merge all of them as "honored dead,"
For they were individual men, one, one,
Their grave a foreign word on a map in red,
A name they saw in a book when child and son,
Or knew first when they hit that beach and ran it.
They only yearned to live in their own land,
To keep a toe hold on a twisting planet
By job and sport and home and loving hand.

They hung their lives on the terrible wall of time
Up which, with face hoping for hope, we climb;
Face where accusing tears no longer fall,
While in their old rooms on the trophied wall
By rod, spiked shoe, girl's head, bent book, the dumb
Mirror waits the face that will not come.

XI

They fought the mighty fury of mass hate,
Uniform, party, group, replacing men,
The tribe abstracted to the absolute state,
Leaders like pigs locked in their filthy pen,
Man a mere number raised to the nth power.
Not only guns, the airman's faceless face,
Tanks, armies, ships, they fought in their doomed hour,
But all yet savage in the human race.

The brag of blood they fought, the brutal sneer
Of racial pride that mocks our mortal feature,
Good love of country heightened to great wrong.
Against that shame, they said for the world to hear,
We've had our human nature far too long
To go back, now, to being merely nature.

XII

Now in the fields ploughed by another's sweat
The native corn is tall. They will not go
To measure it with knee and thigh. But let
No pity cover them like sudden snow.
As Icarus in the fury of his fall
Rose through time to immortality,
So by their savage dying will they all
Live in this long war's monstrous memory.

But they would scrap that little fame to work
One hard hot day under the Kansas glare,
In Illinois, where the low hay mowers jerk,
In Iowa, where corn grows fat on the heat,
Or in the north Red River valley, where
The blond Norwegians harvest the blonder wheat.

XIII

Contrary century
Where men of plain good will
Must cry out—Enemy!
And teach their hands to kill,
Where earth explodes in space
Shamed with its human life,
Where live tears tear the face,
Where wound slashes the knife,

Where men of peace fought back
War-wanting men, and died
Attacking their attack:
As if on those old sands
The spear leapt from Christ's side
To cut the soldier's hands.

XIV

War was evil and they loathed the sight it
Gave to decent men, but worse than war
Was to know evil, and yet not to fight it.
They wanted life, but their own country more.
So learned the killing skill, its bloody ways,
Writing home, when heart and hand were numb:
Heaven and hell we have now in our days,
Earth and the simple living are to come.

So learned, and proved it by death's final scar,
That what we love is what, as men, we are:
Wonder of woman, child and friend, the least
Human good and glory that we try for.
God in the body of a thinking beast,
We are all things we hate, we love, we die for.

XV

Star-staggerer, old earth, through sullen space,
Lost in looking for some absolute light,
Remember, as history lurches toward its night,
The noblest flame is still a human face.
Searching for their lives' terrible truth, they ran
Over earth's water, air, and bloody ground,
On ruthless hill and ravaged city found
Another word for suffering was—man.

A tree stands up, has branches, birds and leaves.
A man stands up, has children, wars and grieves.
Yet anguished, daily life is consecrated
Where men die to defeat an evil hated.
Such death makes luminous the looking eye,
And makes more radiant God's appalled sky.

XVI

Surely when Adam walked through the first trees
The Garden was astonished that a thing,
Upright, with glancing eyes, glad mouth, should tease
Innocent air with a live voice that could sing.
Surely when that first, mortal man had died
Death was astonished that he had a friend
To comfort when he came there terrified,
To give food, drink, on whom he could depend.

But surely death, like these men, is astonished
To find how much hard dying it has taken
To keep a country free, alive, unshaken,
Merely to keep a brutal world admonished
That there are always men willing to die
To keep a plain life, under an open sky.

XVII

War leapt at them—to its astonishment
These men who breathed peace like the common air
Fought back savage and magnificent.
They brought fear to the force that tried to scare.
Animal war they beat down till it whined.
They won that fight although they did not want it.
They beat that beast, as if in sleep the mind
Terrified the dream that came to haunt it.

They battered war by making war, war,
Defeated death, because their dying, dying,
Gave to their country more life, more, more.
Drenched with daylight where the sun dips, dips,
We hear their warning voices crying, crying,
World is a cave where the dark blood drips, drips.

XVIII

Now let our memory of these men make
No form in marble where an artist stood,
But lived-out, rounded rib-cage of a snake
Found perfect in the winter-ruined wood:
Image of nature beautiful in bone
Whose pure curve praises the abandoned breath,
No image like a stutter of bright stone,
But life-delighting shape denoting death.

Remember now their names and their hand's daring,
Whose eyes defied stiff death and left him staring,
Our future life is their memorial
And not bronze language bolted to a wall.
We praise their death by living, not by art,
By proving a free mind and loving heart.

XIX

Casualty, calculated loss,
Dog tag, division, number, date,
The abstract death in triplicate:
From these big words what comes across
Is not men in their natural kindness,
But soldiers, sailors, pilots who,
By chart and luck in the flared night, flew
The bombers in their accurate blindness.

Our words corrupt reality.
The worn, quick syllable of *war*
Proves no blood, terror, agony.
The name of *sorrow* has no more
Night-weeping anguish than the look
Of petals dried in an old book.

XX

Now in the century of clever knowledge
Where the trained mind measures true evidence,
Common sense is still the oldest college:
Wisdom is knowledge of our ignorance.
We trick the atom and teach birds to fly,
Make marvelous machines to make machines,
Cut with our cunning knives the living eye,
Tell the scared mind what each mad terror means.

Yet if these men returned and had their will,
Now, when dark earth through space-like-water dives,
In the great night of the future, they would still
Triangulate the star-drift of their lives
By those fixed points of home they died for: wives,
Table for bread, loved children laughing or ill.

XXI

Rivers were places where they learned to swim,
To fish, to dive for the sand-crawling clam,
But Rhine, Rapido, were places where they learned
To ferry, firing, under fire, to die.
Small towns were places where they learned first names,
Each street and house, and knew the yapping dogs,
But Anzio, St. Lo, were where they learned
Streets could explode and every house could kill.

They learned that war reverses: what was good,
A gentleness, became a deadly flaw,
And what was bad, primitive lust to slay,
Became an honest virtue to be praised.
For our still living grief, it is as if
The scar came first and then the screaming wound.

XXII

Heart of the heartland, where the deep-plowed fields
Lie in huge harvest or the winter-wait,
Where human hope and food are the rich yields,
And nothing there to hate but mortal hate;
Marvelous, hearty, middle country, when
Winds of the world blow dark and full of warning,
Recall, in your great fullness, these dead men,
Homesick for one more live midwestern morning.

So, in a time of fear, have no dejection,
Remember these men on whose lives you stand.
Recall their name, face, human imperfection,
How their death gave life to this lucky land,
For memory is mortal resurrection,
Light as sun rising or a loving hand.

IV

In Praise of Places

IN FLAMING SILKE:

Jamestown, 1607

Those ships float toward us out of rippling time
As they came toward the astonished Indian eye,
Poised on that parted water with no more
Noise than the hang of a hawk on taloned air.

They had followed the sun's gesture of light west
To sail "one of the famousest Rivers that ever
Was found by any Christian," to that place
Named for the English James, where strawberries
Grew four times bigger than in England, where
Such glistering tinctures shone, the very ground
Glowed as if gilded.

Swollen with hope
As their white sails with the shoreward-driving wind,
They knelt on the feverish mud and called their God,
"That tosseth Monarchies and teareth Mountaines."
But then died, half of them, and all men sick,
Hope spilled like vomit on that deadly earth.

Their bodies trailed out of their huts like dogs.
For those who lived, their drink was dirty water,
Their food, upon that lusty soil, a shred
Of rotten meal. That country was to them
"A miserie, a hell, a death, a ruine,"
Four times as dangerous as England.

What
Foolish men to try a furious land:
Goldsmith—they needed iron and the tipped plow.

Perfumer—the smell of honest bread was better.
Jueller—but they needed solid rock
For a fort's walls, not precious stones. Too
Many Gentlemen whose brilliant swords
Harvested no corn.
And in the woods
The subtle savage, wearing a Woolfe head
For Jewell, and gently smoking his stone pipe,
Prettily carved with Bird, a Beare, a Deare,
Sufficient to beat out the brains of a man.

Endured all that, then paid for a wife's crossing,
One hundred and twenty pounds of tobacco each.
No longer bitterly yearned for a horse boiling
In kettles, and on its back their Governor boiling.
Later, Sir Thomas Dale could even say,
He found Jamestown at its daily, usual work,
Bowling in the streets.
"Our cowekeeper here
Of James citty on Sundays goes accoutered
All in freshe flaming silke."
Like bent grass
That springs back from its rubbery root beneath
The foot's weight, out of history that small
Gone town under the weight of human time
Leaps back into this fresh and flaming air.

And now, like Captain Smith, that trusting man,
We lay our head on the rock of the future, knowing
The club will never fall on this green land
While there are in it men like old John Rolfe
Who wrote: "We may truly say in Virginia
We are the most happy people in the world."

CUBAN VOYAGE

A young man growing old, an old man aging,
Walked the white snow-smelling road. You cried:
No more to feel that snarling sadness grab
Body and mind as a dog a bone, to hide
No more that horror in the curved skull raging—

To crash like a car and burn, hear your mouth blab
Honest body pain will can't forbid,
No sneaking ache not even friends can see,
Hope hobbling, whistling like a clubfoot kid,
Pride crawling blindly like the backward crab.

So flew by plane the salt shark-hating sea.
Your eyes filled with salt sea. That city
Tasting like a too ripe foreign fruit.
Air in which the violent light shrieked, Pity!
The cruel ape sorrow climbs him like a tree.

Land where the sugar cane took shallow root,
Land fat with the carrion-eating flower:
Unreal to a pale and northern man the roar
Of burro, parrot, boy in the hot noon hour,
Wanting his winter night, birdless and mute.

A naked, asking land for one who wore
Grief around him like a growing skin,
Too much, too urgent life for one to change
Who still can feel the live blood leaping in
The bold brain, calling still, More, give me more.

Cringed from that livid light you said, In a strange
Country all men become anonymous—
Face with no name, I watch these faces, good
And evil, a human landscape, fabulous
Anguish on anguish climbing, range beyond range.

I thought if, like the vulture, long I stood
Over my life, fed on its living past,
Great grief would nourish me, but now I find,
When youth, mid-years and age are merged at last,
Fear like a child lost in the frantic wood.

Yet not fear only, in this furious place
Where strangling sun coils round me like a rope,
I keep a breathing darkness in my head,
Nor hope for despair as other men for hope,
Trust ice, not fire, my luck, your human face.

Through all that land I followed where you led,
Through fiery valleys, chilled by your despair,
Grateful to learn of grief as a child learns bread,
A native country to you—I was there
Father comforting, son comforted.

REMEMBRANCE

(Translated from Rainer Maria Rilke's "Erinnerung")

You wait, expecting one alone
To make your life grow infinite and new;
The mighty and matchless,
Awakening of stone,
Depths driving toward you.

On bookshelves dark as twilight stand
Volumes in brown and gold;
And you recall a far, long-traveled land,
Pictures, and the clothes
Of twice-lost women you will never hold.

And suddenly you know: it was here!
You rise and face with consternation
An old familiar year
Of pain and prayer and revelation.

MONTAUK WRECK

Sea bangs at the land,
Land booms at the sea.
I lift my looking hand,
My hand glares back at me.

The ocean rages, for
It cannot drag me down.
I rage, that on its floor
Men this long minute drown.

The myriad wave-points gleam
Like trapped and furious flies
Who turn toward me the scream
Of multiple mad eyes.

Men came, where that sea raves,
With line, rod, joke, to look
For fish, but caught the wave's
Barbed and brutal hook.

Dark under chimney stack,
Reckless for light unseen,
They rushed into the black
Underside of green.

Tuna, sea bass, blue,
Were fish names on the lip
With wisecracks at the crew.
Ham sandwich on the hip.

The helicopter hangs,
Loud eye above the beach,
Every wave harangues
The men it cannot reach.

Once men threw in the tide,
Blessed by the robed soothsayer,
God's image, watched it ride
Seaward with threat and prayer.

But these were gods themselves
Whose sport it was to die
For sport on tide's deep shelves,
With shattered human cry.

Friends, family from town,
Angling for news, appear,
The sky bleeds daylight down
On faces bleeding fear.

They fish for the fishermen
Who came, lungs choked with air,
Each city citizen,
To stare at the ocean's stare.

I walk home by those sands
Where fish on fish are fed
To break with symbolic hands
The actual live bread.

V

In Praise

HYMNS FOR THE AGE

I

Lord of each soul and each plain thing,
The heart of man and heart of bread,
You are the One to whom we sing,
Lord of our hand and Lord of head.

From You we take our life and death,
Delight and dread for all our days.
Whether with proud or painful breath,
Still we thank You, still we praise.

Great galaxies of Heaven drift
Like clouds of dust across Your eyes.
Here, with our human voice, we lift
To You our little, living cries.

II

Out of eternity's great dark
God brings in light each mortal soul,
To leap, like an electric spark,
Over the earth from pole to pole.

For time and space are God's great arms
That lift us upward to receive
All that blesses, all that harms,
That make us glad or make us grieve.

For He is everywhere we are,
In rapid mind and running limb,
Or out beyond the farthest star.
Praise God in us that praises Him.

III

Lord, Creator of everything,
The snows and flowers of every year,
The leaf and child, we do not sing
That You are great, but—You are here.

Each living breath will worship You,
Even if wordless: Colors, all
Objects of earth, sad Mary's blue,
Or black mud where the beetles crawl.

God Who is cold and clear in mind,
A green iceberg in a green sea,
God Whom the feeling hand can find,
Although Your face we cannot see.

God, in our houses and our streets,
By midnight moon or midday sun,
We give You a live heart that beats
Because You gave Your living Son.

IV

Father of all, be kind and send us
Grief that is proof of Your great power.
With timeless agony befriend us
That we may know You, hour by hour.

Father Who sees each falling plane,
In time of war each burning city,
Because You watch our sin and pain
We offer You our human pity.

We are the creatures that You made
Imperfect, out of Your perfection.
All that we wait, weak and afraid,
Are Your hard blame and Your direction.

We wait, on earth where we began,
That final day You have begun,
When man in God is God in man,
And Father turns into His Son.

LET THE DEAD GO

Let the dead go as they have let us go.
Why should we call them back with our long cries
Or look for some atoning light below
The gray lids of their light-abandoned eyes?
Do we expect them, pioneers and brave,
Having won continents of dark direction,
To come back chanting, Look! We save! We save!
Their reckless fingers filled with resurrection?

We cling to them as children to the hand
Of father, mother in the frantic night.
But let them go, and let us keep our fears
As something they have lost in their safe land.
Lifc glows in our exuberance of tears.
We turn more human in our mortal fright.

A MODERN ROMANCE:

United States, 1959

Come live with me and be my wife
And we will lead a packaged life,
Where food, drink, fun, all things save pain
Come neatly wrapped in cellophane.

I am the All-American boy,
Certified as fit for joy,
Elected (best of all the breed)
Hairline most likely to recede.
My parchment scroll to verify
Is stamped in gold and witnessed by
Secretary-Treasurer of
Americans Hundred Per Cent For Love.

You are the All-American girl,
Red toe to artificial curl,
Who passed all tests from skipping rope
And using only Cuddly Soap
To making fire in any weather
By rubbing boy and girl together.

We are the nation's nicest team,
Madison Avenue's magic scheme
To show how boy gets girl: my style
Succeeds by using Denta-Smile.

How merchandised that ceremony!
The minister was scrubbed and bony,

And all was sterile in that room
Except, *one* hoped, the eager groom.

Married, with advertising's blessing,
We can begin togethernessing.
Before I carry you, my bride,
Across the threshold and inside,
I'll take, to help my milk-fed bones,
Vitamins, minerals and hormones.

Now look how quickly I have fixed
A dry martini (ready-mixed).
So drink to our day, consecrated,
In chairs of leather, simulated.
While you are changing out of those
Nylon, dacron, rayon clothes,
I cook the dinner, without fail
Proving a real American male,
Humble, without too much endurance,
But lots of paid-up life insurance.

From the deep-freeze, to please your wish,
A TV dinner in its dish,
All ready-seasoned, heat it up.
Pour instant water in this cup
On instant coffee from a can.
Be proud, love, of your instant man.

Innocent food, mechanized manna
(Except the delicate banana),
Can you endure—forgive the question—
The messy horrors of digestion?

Even our love is pasteurized,
Our gentle hope homogenized.

And now our pure, hygienic night.
To our voluptuous delight
Your hair is up, restraints are down,
And cream is patted on your frown.
The brand-name mattress on the bed
Is wrapped in paper like fresh bread.
We can, to make our own campfire,
Turn the electric blanket higher.
We will cry, Darling, I *do* care,
In chastely air-conditioned air.

We've read the books, know what to do,
By science, wife, I offer you
This helpful, vacuum-packed, live nerve
(Just add devotion, dear, and serve).
Hurry! Out back I seem to hear
The landlord's Plymouth prowling near.

If this efficient plan produces
By chance (those awful natural juices!)
That product of a thousand uses,
A Junior, wrapped in elastic
Inexpensive bag of plastic
(Just break the seal and throw away)
From antiseptic throats we'll say:
It was an All-American day.

THE PANTHER

(Translated from Rainer Maria Rilke's "Der Panther")

From going always over bars his glance
Holds nothing more, grown tired, as if there hurled
Against him but a thousand bars' expanse—
Beyond a thousand bars no other world.

The wary walking of the strong stride, dark
Around the littlest circle of his land
Is like a dance of power around an arc
Where, stupefied, a mighty Will may stand.

Only sometimes the live lid of the eye
Lifts, and an image enters quietly,
Travels the taut, tight limbs without a cry
And ceases, in the heart, to be.

AN OLD PALESTINIAN DONKEY

I'd rather carry loads of olive wood
Or jugs of wine, than a man, for they won't trick you.
They'll bend your back, you'll carry more than you should,
But a man will jerk your mouth, and swear and kick you.

But once I took a man down streets paved with palms,
And crowds of people yelling, packed in tightly.
Slowly I walked. He smiled as they sang psalms.
His hand was soft on my mouth. He rode lightly.

He wasn't a governor; although that crowd
Screamed, it was honest praise and not plain fear.
He wasn't a general; although they bowed,
There wasn't a soldier to threaten with his spear.

Head up, ears straight, I carried that man well.
(A donkey has his stubborn little pride.)
Who was he? Where did he go? I cannot tell.
He never came back to *me* for another ride.

I suppose he's a shepherd now, counting sheep,
Or lost in the wars, a sword-scooped hole for a grave,
Or farmer scanning the sky before his sleep,
Or dragged to Imperial Rome, a galley slave.

I had a gray colt trotting by my side,
Nudging into my ribs, scared of the noise.
Maybe it's trudging somewhere now, its hide
Itching, overloaded, beaten by boys.

And look what's happened to me: my hoofs are chipped,
My ears (they were handsome once) are raw and torn.
My old bones ache, and yesterday I slipped
And gashed my shoulders in a patch of thorn.

I've carried children, pine roots, every load
In sand and stone, wherever donkeys go.
But still my back rides lightly where he rode,
The fur is cross-shaped and it seems to glow.

ABOUT THE AUTHOR

PAUL ENGLE was born in Cedar Rapids, Iowa, in 1908. Following graduation from Coe College, he studied at the University of Iowa, Columbia University, and at Oxford as a Rhodes Scholar, where he rowed for Merton College both at Oxford and in the International Regattas at Marlowe and Henley.

Mr. Engle's first volume of poems, *Worn Earth,* was his M.A. thesis at the University of Iowa and was also the Yale University Press Prize book for 1932. His second book of verse was *American Song,* which had a large public success and included the poem "America Remembers," selected by *Poetry* magazine to represent the Chicago Century of Progress. Succeeding works of poetry included *Break the Heart's Anger* (1936), *Corn* (1938), *West of Midnight* (1941), *American Child* (1945), an expanded version of *American Child* (1956), and *The Word of Love* (1951). Mr. Engle is also the author of *Always the Land,* a novel about people and horses in Iowa. He was for six years editor of the annual collection of O. Henry Prize Stories.

At present, Mr. Engle is director of the internationally famous creative writing program at the University of Iowa, where he has been on the faculty since 1937. He is married and has two daughters, Mary and Sara, about whom his volume *American Child* and the poems on children in POEMS IN PRAISE were written.